T0088407

Dance Caprice

by Christopher Bunting

for Cello and Piano

Oxford University Press

For D.L.

DANCE - CAPRICE

CHRISTOPHER BUNTING

© Oxford University Press 1965

Printed in Great Britain
OXFORD UNIVERSITY PRESS, MUSIC DEPARTMENT, GREAT CLARENDON STREET, OXFORD OX2 6DP

Photocopying this copyright material is ILLEGAL.

CELLO

For D.L.

DANCE - CAPRICE

Allegro, energico

CHRISTOPHER BUNTING

Notes for Cellist

1. Play bar 1, and similar figures, at the heel.
2. Play bar 7, and similar, detaché, in the middle of the bow.
3. Play 14 from left to right, [also bars 82-5]
4. Play bars 22-26 at the heel.
5. Play 55-6 at the heel, slightly nearer the fingerboard than usual.

© Oxford University Press 1965

Printed in Great Britain
OXFORD UNIVERSITY PRESS, MUSIC DEPARTMENT, GREAT CLARENDON STREET, OXFORD OX2 6DP

Photocopying this copyright material is ILLEGAL.

19
f pesante
25
mp
31
37
mf
f
mf
secco

43
8va
crescendo
f
49
8
55
ff
Grazioso e pochissimo meno mosso
mf
8
8va
pp
61
poco a poco al tempo primo
f
8va
mp

Processed and printed by
Halstan & Co. Ltd., Amersham, Bucks., England

ISBN 978-0-19-355750-5